I Like Myself

Written by Graciela Castellanos
and illustrated by Cristina Gil

I like myself
and what I see.

I like
my eyes,
my face
and my hair.

I like
my ears,
my mouth
and my nose.

I like my family and...

my friends.

I like it when I smile.

I like it when I can help many
and please some others.

I like it when
I'm strong and brave,
smart and nice.

I like it when I play,

when I do
what I like to do.

I like it when I share
and care,

and I give my love to...

you,
you,
and you.

More books by Graciela Castellanos

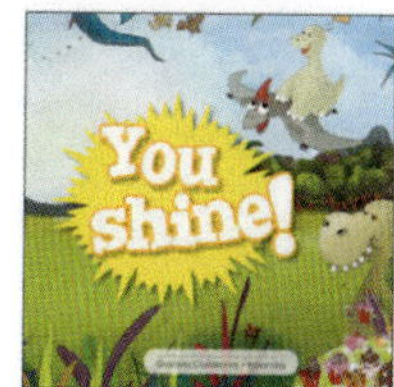

Printed in Great Britain
by Amazon.co.uk, Ltd.,
Marston Gate.